Michael Barrymore's

KidS SaY THE FUNNIEST ThingS

Michael Barrymore's
Kids Say The Funniest Things

Edited By
Geoff Tibballs

GRANADA

The production team on *Kids Say The Funniest Things* are:
Nigel Lythgoe, Maurice Leonard, Russell Norman, Kevin Hubbard,
Liz Minchin, Malcolm Donkin, Lee Connolly, Claire Jenkinson, Camilo De La
Huerta, Susan Warwicker, Adele Dewison, Jane Cotton and Gary Brooks.

The *Kids Say The Funniest Things* team would like to thank
the following people for all their kind help:
Wendy Max, Mrs Devina Cannon, press officer of The Pony Club, The Patchwork
Theatre Group (Juniors), Henry Ibberson and Gladys Jones, Miss Becky Hobbs
of Lethbridge Junior School, Swindon, and the children from Lethbridge Junior
School, Swindon, Sue Dale and The Blue and White Rope Skippers, Matthew
McGuirk, Richard Smith, Arthur Green, Sonsha Smith and Camile Hamilton.

First published in 2000 by Granada Media
an imprint of André Deutsch Ltd
in association with
Granada Media Group
76 Dean Street
London W1V 5HA
www.vci.co.uk

Michael Barrymore's Kids Say The Funniest Things
is a London Weekend Television Production

The right of Geoff Tibballs to be identified as the author of this work has been
asserted by him in accordance with the Copyright, Designs and Patents Act 1988

A catalogue record for this book is available from the British Library

ISBN 0 233 99752 0

Printed and bound in the UK by
Butler & Tanner Ltd, Frome and London

1 3 5 7 9 10 8 6 4 2

Design by Design 23

Contents

Foreword

The only thing you can be sure of getting when you ask a child a question on TV is an honest answer. For kids are notoriously unpredictable. They can go shy on you or they can be outrageously candid, telling nine million people all the things their Mums and Dads have been trying to keep secret for the past 20 years. Kids are spontaneous – they invariably say the first thing that comes into their head. You couldn't script their replies if you wanted to.

And that's the beauty of *Kids Say The Funniest Things* – it's all so natural, so unrehearsed. But while the answers may be innocent, they are often remarkably sharp. A TV presenter underestimates kids at his peril. They may look as if butter wouldn't melt in their mouths, but they can make fools of you in seconds. For that's another great thing about kids. Whereas adults might gawp at you if they've seen you on the telly, kids just wade in and say what they think. As you will see from this book, I've certainly been put in my place a few times on the show.

This book features the most hilarious moments from the first two series – not only exchanges that you saw on screen, but also some of the out-takes and moments that didn't quite make it into the final programmes. The result is a wonderful insight into a child's mind on such diverse subjects as their family, boyfriends and girlfriends, animals, famous people, likes and dislikes, God, and what they want to do when they're older. I hope as you read through it you will have a good laugh and thank God that children are the way they are. And I hope you'll agree with me that kids really do say the funniest things.

Happy Families

Kids think Mums and Dads are put on earth just to make their lives a misery. Or could it be the other way round?

Judge for yourselves as you hear about parents with more skeletons in their cupboards than The Addams Family...

olly Williams, aged 7

Barrymore: *Where's your Dad?*
Dwayne: *He lives at home with his Mum. Big baby.*
Barrymore: *Did Mummy tell you that?*
Dwayne: *Yea.*
Barrymore: *I had a feeling she had!*
Dwayne Lennon, aged 10, from Brockley, London

Barrymore: *You've got a lovely smile. Has Mummy got a lovely smile?*
Zoe: *Not when she takes her false teeth out.*
Zoe Slater, aged 8, from Edinburgh

Barrymore: *What's the best thing about your Dad?*
Rhys: *Sometimes, when I'm not looking at him, my Dad puts his hand under my bottom, nips it and says it's Jock the Croc!*
Rhys Hodnett, aged 7, from Cardiff

Azanya Byer-Andrews, aged 6

Dad's a Jock – he speaks with a Scottish accent in Scotland and an English accent in England.
Callum Weston, aged 7, from Yeovil

Barrymore: *Have Mummy and Daddy any bad habits?*
Lacy: *When my Dad pumps, he never says 'Pardon me!'*
Lacy Cartwright, aged 9, from West Lothian

Barrymore: *What happened the last time you came to London?*
Dominic: *They asked me about Grandad, and he's got dirty habits.*
Barrymore: *What sort?*
Dominic: *His favourite thing is to eat cat food.*
Dominic Moore, aged 5

Mohima Akthar, aged 6

Mum picks her nose all the time and flicks it in the bin.
Jack Bell, aged 7, from St Ives

Dad thinks pointing at his ears is dancing.
Megan McGuire, aged 4, from Glasgow

Dad brakes too hard in the car and his feet smell.
Kate Burrows, aged 6, from Havant

Saima Begum, aged 6

Right:
Tara Hinton, aged 7

Dilwar Hussain,
aged 6

Mum drinks tea all the time and is not allowed to go to the gym.
Benjamin Sadler, aged 4, from Harrogate

My Mum waxes my Auntie's arms when she's got loads of hair on them.
Jordan Melius, aged 7, from London

Barrymore: *What do Mummy and Daddy do at home?*
Megan: *Just argue.*
Megan McGuire, aged 4, from Glasgow

Barrymore: *Do Mummy and Daddy ever fall out at home?*
Daniel: *Yes, a lot.*
Barrymore: *What do they fall out about, Daniel?*
Daniel: *My Dad cracking an egg on my Mum's head!*
Daniel Shenton, aged 6, from Solihull

Mum always shouts at Dad 'cos she has to look after those pesky kids.
Clayton Fernley, aged 6, from Milton Keynes

Mum is always shouting at Dad because he does nothing.
Megan Corfield, aged 5, from Swinton

Mummy always gets cross with Daddy because he doesn't wipe my bottom properly.
Harry Alexander, aged 4, from Preston

Mum found Dad at BT. She was his boss and bossed him around, but now Dad bosses Mum around. When she points at him with her finger, he threatens to break it off.
Tamsyn Whitchurch, aged 7, from north Somerset

Mum and Dad shout a lot at each other. They think I can't hear when they're saying rude words, but really I'm popping my ear round my bedroom door.
Rhys Hodnett, aged 7, from Cardiff

Mum shouts and laughs at Dad through slit eyes.
Robin Cunningham, aged 5, from Manchester

Anu Olukoga, aged 6

Michelle Elizabeth
Hinojosa Bastidas,
aged 6

My mummy
by Michelle
age 6.

My Mum is funny and has smelly feet which she puts in my face. The smell is so bad, it knocks me off the sofa.
Jake Thomas, aged 8, from Cardiff

Mum is always buying me presents all year round and does massive burps at the dinner table and in shops.
Maxwell Monro, aged 7, from Harrow

Mum dropped an iron on her finger, 'cos she is dozy.
Adam Davies, aged 7, from Liverpool

Aysha J., aged 6

Mum snores like a cow, but she doesn't moo.
Liam Colmer, aged 6, from Waterlooville

I can hear my Dad snoring from my bedroom and he is two staircases away.
Alicia Jauffret, aged 5, from London

We call Dad 'Homer' after Homer Simpson because he walks around in just his underpants and reads women's magazines.
Tamsyn Whitchurch, aged 7, from north Somerset

When it's party-time, Dad drinks loads of beer and my Uncle Graham drinks hundreds of beers, then gets drunk and wibble wobbles and falls over.
Joshua Smeed, aged 5, from Portsmouth

When England played Argentina, Mum drank three bottles of wine – mostly red, though she does drink quite a bit of white. Then she was very hungover and had to ask, 'Where's the toilet?', 'cos she couldn't see, and she was not very well.
Callum Weston, aged 7, from Yeovil

Dad always goes to the pub on the bus. He drinks 59 pints and gets very drunk.
Samuel Hather, aged 4, from Halifax

When Dad is too drunk, he lets Mum drive.
Callum Miller, aged 8, from Birmingham

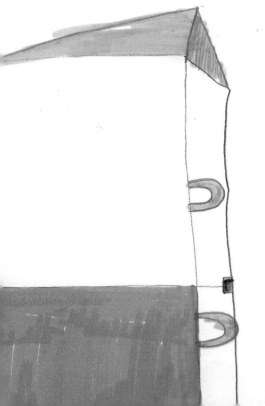

Nazmin, aged 6

We live in an inn really – not a pub, 'cos a pub is where naughty people go and an inn is where the nice people go.
Adnam Turner, aged 6, from Luddesdowne

Dad is always in a temper when he drives, 'cos he hates women drivers, who he says shouldn't be allowed on the road. When Dad was waiting for a bus once, he did not want to get on it when it came, 'cos it had a woman driver.
Adam Davies, aged 7, from Liverpool

Barrymore: *What's Mummy like in the car?*
Patrick: *She's rubbish at driving, but me Dad's like uh-oh, coppers are after us, better put foot down!*
Patrick Doran, aged 7, from Sheffield

Barrymore: *Is your Mum very young?*
Gareth: *Bit old sometimes.*
Barrymore: *In what way is she old then?*
Gareth: *She hits me on the head sometimes.*
Barrymore: *How old's your Granny?*
Gareth: *About 55.*
Barrymore: *Do you think 55 is very old then?*
Gareth: *Yeah.*
Barrymore: *What about Grandad? What's he like?*
Gareth: *65. He chases squirrels all the time.*
Gareth Fient, aged 5, from Kent

Barrymore: *If you had £1,000, what would you spend it on?*
Zoe: *I'd buy a horse and throw my Mum and Dad in the bin.*
Zoe Slater, aged 8, from Edinburgh

Barrymore: *What does Daddy do when he's at home?*
Elizabeth: *He hides behind the door on Sunday morning when I'm in my nightie and he jumps out from behind the door, and I scream my head off and fall over.*
Barrymore: *Has your Daddy got a nickname for you?*
Elizabeth: *Stinker.*
Elizabeth Hathaway-White, aged 7, from Birmingham

When Mummy was ill, Daddy cooked once and made a big mess – baked beans and eggs went everywhere. But Mum was too ill to see.
Natalie Glew, aged 8, from Lincolnshire

Grandad is a fattie, who eats like a pig. Gran is an old hag. Mum is a good Mum, but she could improve!
Jake Thomas, aged 8, from Cardiff

I like Nanny's teeth when she takes them out.
Benjamin Sadler, aged 4, from Harrogate

I'd like to strangle my brother with a python so I can have his bed!
Jake Heal, aged 5, from Bristol

I love my sister Daniella, but I like to make her jump!
Tristian Hill, aged 6, from Swansea

Tamsyn, my sister, is Miss Perfect and she should be a vicar.
Tiffany Whitchurch, aged 7, from north Somerset

Barrymore: *Do you think your sister loves you?*
Bobbie: *No!*
Bobbie Burgess, aged 8, from London

My sister Demi is scared of the dark and wants you to sleep with her, but she snores.
Christopher Holwell, aged 8, from Hemel Hempstead

My sister Lisa is 13 and can cross her eyes.
Ben Russell, aged 7, from Leeds

Ali: *When Daddy's at work, Mum just watches TV.*
Barrymore: *What did she say when you said you might be talking about her on the show?*
Ali: *She said, 'If you say anything about me on that show, I'm going to kill you when you come home.'*
Barrymore: *What sort of things do you know about Mum?*
Ali: *She's got a boyfriend and she says, 'You just pretend to everyone that he's my cousin, OK?'*
Barrymore: *Has Daddy got a girlfriend?*
Ali: *No.*
Barrymore: *Do you think he'll get a girlfriend eventually?*
Ali: *No.*
Barrymore: *Why don't you think he'll get a girlfriend?*
Ali: *Too ugly.*
Ali Dowlatshah, aged 7, from Glasgow

Michael Barrymore

The Working Day

Mums and Dads are always going on about how hard they work, but do kids really believe them...?

Barrymore: *What do your Mum and Dad do?*
Dominic: *Argue.*
Barrymore: *What do they argue about?*
Dominic: *My Dad always says when he's been out he had to do all the work.*
Barrymore: *Overtime?*
Dominic: *Yeah.*
Barrymore: *He was doing extra work? He wasn't out on the town?*
Dominic: *Yeah.*
Barrymore: *Maybe he's right.*
Dominic: *Well, they just kiss and make up after that.*
Dominic Creighton, aged 8, from Blackpool

My Mummy does work in the back room. She always does it upstairs and downstairs.
Harry Alexander, aged 4, from Preston

My Mum never gets out of bed in the morning. She's too lazy.
Elizabeth Hathaway-White, aged 7, from Birmingham

My Mum loves to sleep. I call her 'Sleepyhead Mum'. Sometimes, if you shout, 'The patio door's on fire!' she wakes up.
Peri Ozkeskin, aged 7, from Essex

Dad falls asleep on the settee and trumps. Mum does ironing, shopping, cooking, everything, while me Dad just sleeps.
Patrick Doran, aged 7, from Sheffield

My Dad is literally sleep and eat, like the cat. He also farts and burps.
Hannah Joshua, aged 7, from Cardiff

My Dad works in a bank. He sits on his bum all day.
Anthony Duffy, aged 6, from Liverpool

My Daddy goes to work, but he doesn't actually do some work – he just eats biscuits and plays on the computer.
Mariella Hiscock, aged 5, from Chesterfield

My Dad works at a butcher's, but he's been sacked. He spends more time at the gym than what he does with my Mum. Dad wants Mum to think that he's stronger than her, but he's not.
Dominic Creighton, aged 8, from Blackpool

My Dad's an auctioneer – he sells china, furniture and all sods and bobs.
Samuel Davies, aged 8, from Sutton

Dad's in the AA. Well, I don't know what it stands for, do I? He never told me.
Hannah Joshua, aged 7, from Cardiff

Juned, aged 6

Mum works in a newsagents. She has a very stinky woman customer who doesn't cut her toenails.
Christopher Holwell, aged 8, from Hemel Hempstead

Mum can't handle me all day because she has cleaning and cooking to do. Besides, Mum has all the soaps to watch on TV.
Chantelle Douglas, aged 8, from Bristol

Mum goes to work and helps people go to bed because they are lazy.
Kate Burrows, aged 6, from Havant
(Her Mum is a part-time care worker)

Mum cuts hair, then she washes it, then blow-dries it and then everyone goes home, and the shop is closed.
Natasha Greene, aged 5, from Harrow Weald
(Her Mum is a hairdresser)

Barrymore: *Who works the hardest out of your Mum and Dad?*
Samuel: *My Dad.*
Barrymore: *Why's that?*
Samuel: *Because he has to sell the stuff.*
Barrymore: *But Mummy has to look after the home.*
Samuel: *Yeah, but my Dad pays the mortgage.*
Samuel Davies, aged 8, from Sutton

Dad works with people whose brains have gone crazy from accidents.
Natalie Chua, aged 7, from Bletchley
(Her Dad is a psychiatric nurse)

Mizanur Rahman Masum, aged

—mum

Sweet

Juned, aged 6

Barrymore: *What does Mummy do?*
Kurtis: *She used to work for Lloyd's Bank. Now she works for me and my brother at home.*
Kurtis Campbell, aged 5, from Kennington

Barrymore: *What do your Mum and Dad do?*
Jordan: *My Dad's got a bald head.*
Barrymore: *And what does he do with it?*
Jordan: *He shaves it every time.*
Jordan Melius, aged 7, from London

Barrymore: *What do Mummy and Daddy do?*
Ryan: *Sometimes they smack me.*
Ryan Archibald, aged 4, from Scotland

Barrymore: *Does Mummy earn more than Daddy?*
Hannah: *Well, I'd say she does a bit, 'cos Dad's quite lazy.*
Hannah Joshua, aged 7, from Cardiff

Monisha Sahni, aged 6

Kissing
And
Stuff

**Boys and girls
come out to play.
But what goes on when
teacher's not looking?**

And where exactly
do babies come from?
We asked our
panel of experts...

Barrymore: *What's your Mummy got in her tummy?*
Adam: *A baby ... and some food.*
Barrymore: *And how did the baby get in her tummy?*
Adam: *The doctor put it in.*
Adam Norton, aged 4 (whose Mum was pregnant)

Babies come from the sky and Mummies go up to the sky to choose a baby, then they bring a baby back in their tummies. It is not born on the same day, but about one million days later!
Aimee Reynolds, aged 5, from Wakefield

Barrymore: *Your Mummy's got a baby in her tummy at the moment. Do you know how it gets there?*
Jordan: *Well, my Mum's got an egg in her belly and some fishes. And my Dad's got some liquid.*
Jordan Thorpe, aged 4, from Eltham

Mummy got me when David put a seed in her – it was red when it was growing.
Ashley Florio, aged 6, from New Milton

Barrymore: *Do you know how babies are born?*
Christopher: *Tadpoles.*
Christopher Walsh, aged 10, from Mitcham, Surrey

Barrymore: *Do you know how Mummy has babies?*
Daniel: *She just cracks an egg inside her body.*
Daniel Shenton, aged 6, from Solihull

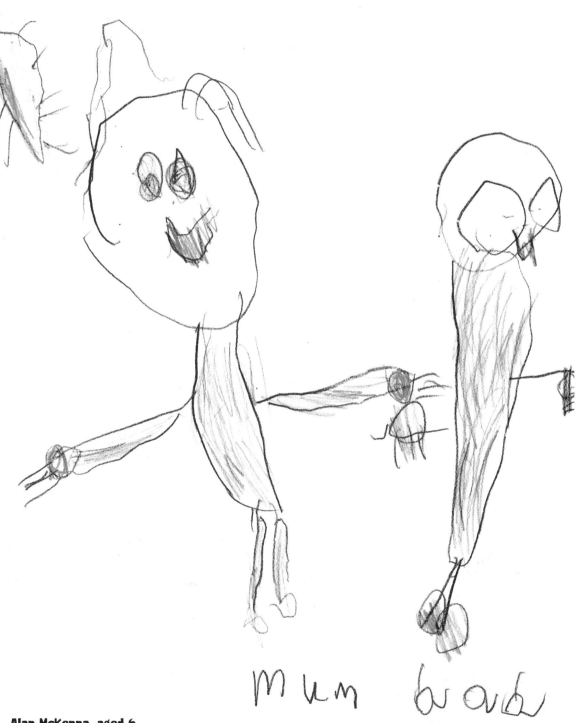

Alan McKenna, aged 6

Barrymore: *What do you like about your girlfriend Laura?*
Christopher: *She doesn't get angry with me if I accidentally hit her.*
Barrymore: *Have you kissed her yet?*
Christopher: *Yes.*
Barrymore: *Was it nice?*
Christopher: *Yes.*
Barrymore: *Did Laura like it?*
Christopher: *Mmm, no.*
Christopher Miller, aged 7, from Scotland

I've got six girlfriends – or seven, or maybe four. Some days they love me and some days they don't!
George Edwards, aged 7, from Hornchurch

Kisses are disgusting because they are so wet. They come from the inside of your mouth – that is why they are wet.
Eluned Williams, aged 4, from Cardiff

Barrymore: *Do you like girls?*
Dominic: *No. I like kissing them.*
Dominic Moore, aged 5

I've got three girlfriends – Chloe, Becca and Paignton. They are all coming to live in my house. Becca and Chloe are going to sleep with me and Paignton can sleep on the sofa.
Connor Small, aged 4, from Portsmouth

Jessica Haddigan, aged 8

Charlie Watkin, aged 6

I've got 100 boyfriends, but Thomas Lloyd is my number one favourite. I kissed him on the cheek at the pub.
Aimee Reynolds, aged 5, from Wakefield

I love Vicky, my girlfriend, because she is kind and generous, and I join in her games and she helps the bin lady.
Callum Weston, aged 7, from Yeovil

Barrymore: *Do you like boys?*
Jessica: *No, they stink.*
Jessica Martin, aged 7, from Croydon

Barrymore: *Have you got a girlfriend?*
Nathan: *Yes, Laura.*
Barrymore: *And do you want to have children when you grow up?*
Nathan: *Yes, 25.*
Nathan Day, aged 6, from Rotherham

My boyfriend is Jack. He is always trying to kiss me. He has asked me to marry him. I said 'Yes' and hope to have 18 children.
Bernice Lister, aged 4, from Knaresborough

I don't like girls – they're always chasing after me and trying to kiss me.
Samuel Hather, aged 4, from Halifax

I've got 45 million girlfriends, but can only remember one.
Adnam Turner, aged 6, from Luddesdowne

Hafsa Khanom, aged 6

Barrymore: *Have you got a girlfriend?*
Gareth: *Only me Mum.*
Gareth Fient, aged 5

Jodie, aged 6

I will never get married because women might want you to wash the pots.
Elute Roberts, aged 8, from Manchester

I haven't got a girlfriend, but I want one when I am 28 so she can do the housework and cook and clean.
Callum Miller, aged 8, from Birmingham

Boys are far too smelly.
Kate Burrows, aged 6, from Havant

I haven't got a boyfriend 'cos I gave them all to my friend. I hate boys 'cos they think they are really sexy.
Nicole Goodchild, aged 6, from Cockfosters

Hannah Arbon, aged 8

My boyfriend, Joe, is a bit naughty and I would like to slip some love potion into his food so he will like me more.
Aisha Weise-Forbes, aged 7, from Plumstead

I dumped my girlfriend 'cos she was always bossing me around.
Ben Russell, aged 7, from Leeds

I don't have a girlfriend. Girls want to take all your money all the time.
Jake Heal, aged 5, from Bristol

I had a girlfriend but she didn't stop hugging and kissing me.
Robin Cunningham, aged 5, from Manchester

I have a girlfriend at school called Hannah and I love her, but I still like Melanie from EastEnders.
Vincent Riley, aged 4, from Hove

I've only got one or two boyfriends. I don't want to marry any of them in case they are vampires.
Megan Corfield, aged 5, from Swinton

Kimberly Wilson, aged 6

I've got four girlfriends. One said she loves me and that I had to turn around, the next one started shouting at me, and the third one keeps on trying to carry me and make me sit on her. And the fourth one doesn't really like me.
Kurtis Campbell, aged 5, from Kennington

Barrymore: *Have you got a girlfriend?*
Dean: *Yeah, I did, but she moved on me.*
Barrymore: *How often did you go out with her?*
Dean: *Four days a week.*
Barrymore: *And she's moved away? Has it upset you?*
Dean: *Half and half, really.*
Barrymore: *What do you mean, half and half?*
Dean: *It a bit upset me, it a bit didn't.*
Barrymore: *What did you like about her?*
Dean: *The way she made me laugh and that.*
Barrymore: *How did she make you laugh?*
Dean: *Saying funny things.*
Barrymore: *What sort of things did she used to say to you?*
Dean: *I haven't got the slightest idea.*
Barrymore: *Do you find life confusing?*
Dean: *Half and half again.*
Barrymore: *What sort of milk do you like?*
Dean: *I like it plain, but not semi-skimmed.*
Barrymore: *Sort of half and half? Do you think you'll ever get married?*
Dean: *I don't know yet.*
Barrymore: *You may get married or you may not get married ...*
Dean: *Yeah. That's not half and half.*
Barrymore: *What do you think about that girl there?*
Dean: *Mmm. Half and half.*
Dean Pye, aged 9, from Manchester

I have two boyfriends – Angus and Mark. Mark is sillier and Angus is silly because he pretends to be dead and then comes alive again.
Alicia Jauffret, aged 5, from London

Babies look like aliens first.
Christopher Walsh, aged 10, from Mitcham, Surrey

Love is silly and shouldn't be in our world. You can give people a hug and say 'Can't wait to see you', but no sloppy kisses!
Elute Roberts, aged 8, from Manchester

Barrymore: *What kind of girls do you like?*
Christopher: *Blonde hair, blue eyes, sexy legs.*
Christopher Walsh, aged 10, from Mitcham, Surrey

Barrymore: *Do you have a girlfriend, Harry?*
Harry: *Yeah.*
Barrymore: *Do you love her?*
Harry: *Yeah.*
Barrymore: *And are you going to get married?*
Harry: *Yeah.*
Barrymore: *Do you want any children?*
Harry: *Mmm, yeah.*
Barrymore: *How many?*
Harry: *Mmm, 81.*
Barrymore: *Looks like your Mum's got a lot of nails to do, doesn't it?*
Harry Alexander, aged 4, from Preston
(His Mum is a manicurist)

Blonde hair, nice big blue eyes, and no goofy teeth.
Dean Pye, aged 9, from Manchester (on his ideal girl)

When Mum kisses me, I turn into an ice cube and smile.
Nathan Harrison, aged 6, from West Yorkshire

Mum is a floozy just like my sister, 'cos she has loads of boyfriends. At parties she always snogs her boyfriend.
Ben Russell, aged 7, from Leeds

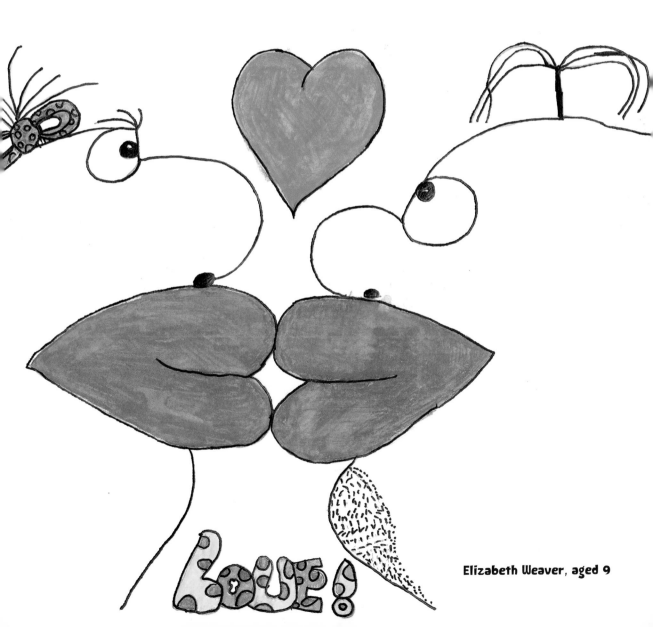

Elizabeth Weaver, aged 9

Samuel: *When my Dad's driving, he takes my Mum's hand and kisses her on the hand.*
Barrymore: *And what does your Mum say?*
Samuel: *She says, 'Get off, you're just annoying me!'*
Samuel Davies, aged 8, from Sutton

Daddy squashes Mummy, 'cos he rolls about in bed.
Daniel Baines, aged 4, from Ashstead

Mum and Dad bounce around on their bed, and roll round and round and round, kissing. Dad sleeps with a T-shirt on and his pants off.
Natalie Chua, aged 7, from Bletchley

Matthew: *Mummy and Daddy take their clothes off when they go in the bath together.*
Barrymore: *Well, that's all right – Mummies and Daddies can do that.*
Matthew: *But he looks at Mummy's rude parts.*
Matthew Jackson, aged 6

Barrymore: *When your Mum and Dad are in the bedroom, have you ever heard them fighting in there?*
Dominic: *They sound like two dogs.*
Dominic Creighton, aged 8, from Blackpool

Mum and Dad share a room and, guess what, they sleep together.
Eluned Williams, aged 4, from Cardiff

Mimi, aged 3

When Dad gets very fierce, Mum stamps upstairs and lies on her bed.
Then Dad goes upstairs and says something and they kiss and talk, and
then they start rowing again.
Shelby Murray, aged 5, from Bristol

Barrymore: *What do you hear from your Mum and Dad?*
Jessica: *Have you got a woman yourself?*
Jessica Martin, aged 7, from Croydon

All Creatures Great And Small

Things you didn't know about animals from some budding David Attenboroughs...

Billy Allsep, aged 6

Manish Maharjan, aged 6

• *All elephants are called Nellie.*

• *Penguins eat Fish, but where do they get chips?*

• *These penguins have not got wrappers.*

• *These penguins remind me of Michael Barrymore.*

• *Penguins came to London because it was too cold in the North Pole.*

• *A pelican can't talk because it's got some babies in its mouth.*

• *Pelicans drop babies down the chimney, I think.*

• *When you see pelicans, you've got to cross the road.*

• *A camel's got legs like Tina Turner.*

• *Elephants have long memories because they've got big heads.*

• *I think a rhinoceros is faster than Linford Christie.*

• *I wonder if giraffes wake up with stiff necks.*

• *Giraffes are cheeky 'cos they've got a lot of neck.*

• *A leopard never changes his socks.*

Barrymore: *What happened to your hamster?*
Thomas: *I dropped it down the toilet. I wanted to get rid of her poohs.*
Thomas Blake, aged 5, from Berkshire

Dad shouts at me when I'm not watching the dog, 'cos it poops and wees everywhere.
Jack Bell, aged 7, from St Ives

Barrymore: *Do you know what monkeys do?*
Gareth: *I know that they eat bananas all the time.*
Gareth Fient, aged 5, from Kent

Barrymore: *Got any pets?*
Daniel: *Three goldfish.*
Barrymore: *What are their names?*
Daniel: *Gareth Southgate, Lee Hendrie and Dion Dublin.*
Daniel Morley, aged 7, from Birmingham

Johnn, aged 6

Avanghan Jennifer Watkins,
aged 9

Heidi Luckhurst,
aged 10

!Josha the Giragge!

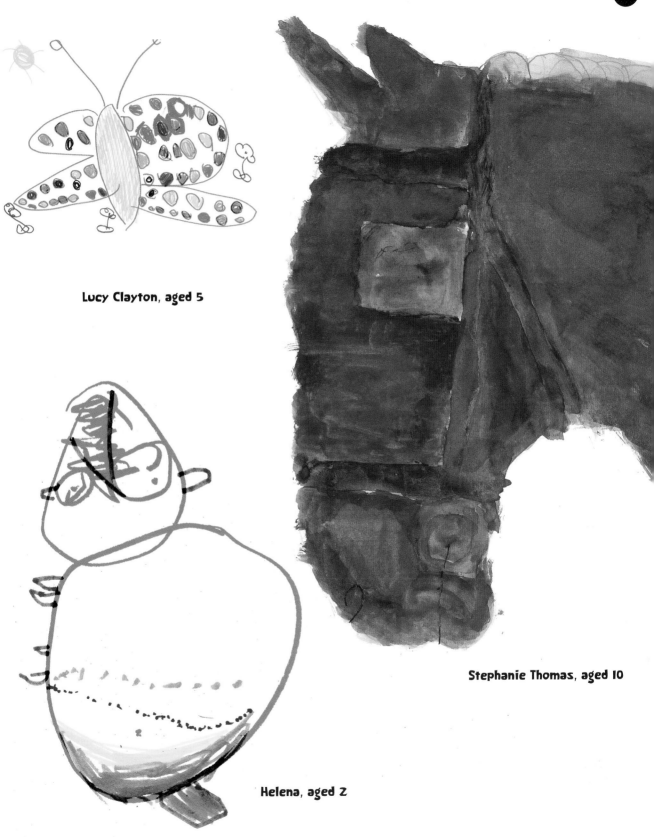

Lucy Clayton, aged 5

Stephanie Thomas, aged 10

Helena, aged 2

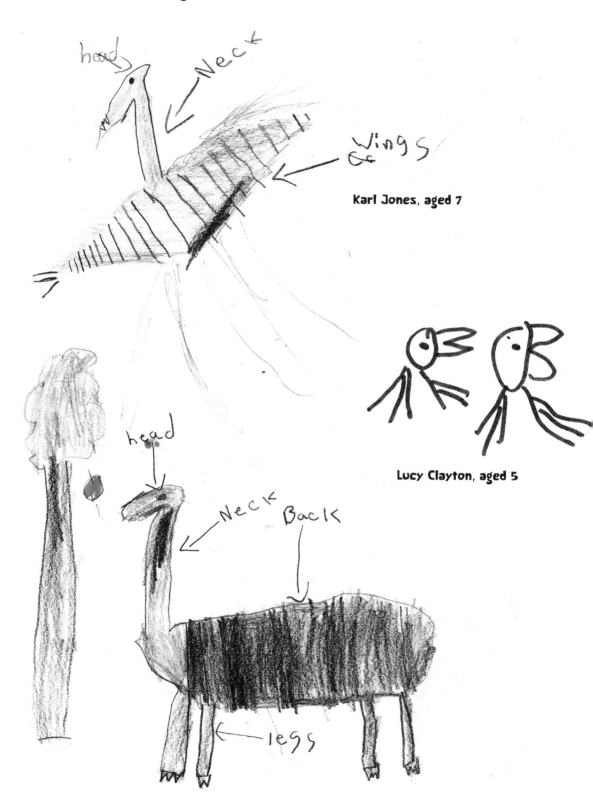

had

Neck

Wings

Karl Jones, aged 7

Lucy Clayton, aged 5

head

Neck

Back

legs

these are dinorsvars.

I've got two fish, but Mum won't let me feed them so they end up starving.
Megan Corfield, aged 5, from Swinton

Barrymore: *Have you got any pets?*
Tyronne: *I had five fish.*
Barrymore: *You had five fish? And what happened to them?*
Tyronne: *They all died. The first one what died was black and kept on squeezing to the top and being greedy.*
Barrymore: *Did you bury the fish?*
Tyronne: *No – just chucked them out.*
Tyronne Alexander-Jarrett, aged 7, from London

Lucy Clayton, aged 5

Fiona Johnston, aged 10

Manish Maharjan, aged 6

Mum and Dad like to eat fish, but you have to be careful you don't eat too many otherwise there will be no baby fish. I've got four guinea pigs – all girls. We had to take the boy one away because I didn't want the boy one anywhere near the girl ones.
Eluned Williams, aged 4, from Cardiff

Gus Allen, aged 6

Right: Samantha Connelly, aged 10

I used to have a hamster, but my sister dropped it and it died.
Christopher Holwell, aged 8, from Hemel Hempstead

Barrymore: *I've got a Jack Russell, but it's never barked.*
Christopher: *What? Has it miaowed?*
Christopher Walsh, aged 10, from Mitcham, Surrey

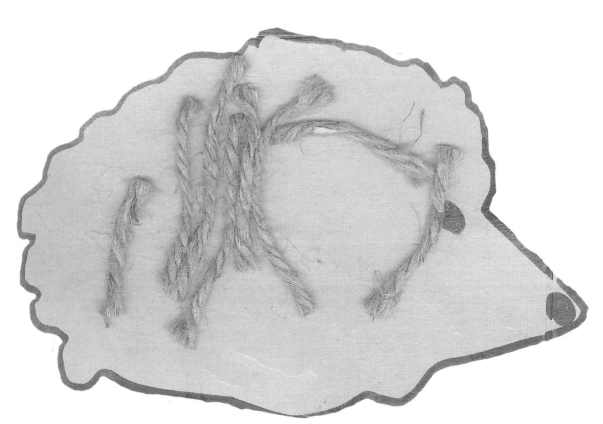

Mimi, aged 3

Rhys English, aged 6

tummy

teeth

NeX

legs

Lee, aged 6

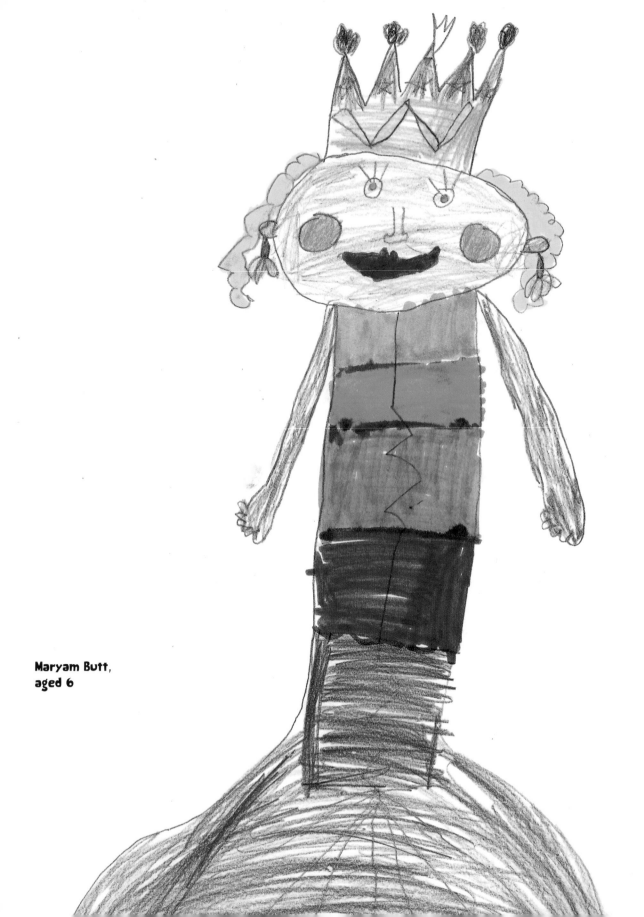

Maryam Butt,
aged 6

People In Power

Forget
Andrew Morton –
it's kids who know
what really goes
on inside
Buckingham
Palace...

I think the Queen's favourite food is cabbage.

●

She's got three boys and a girl, but I'm not sure if she's got a husband.

●

She's got two children and one's called Prince Philip. When Prince Philip is naughty, she sends him to bed.

●

She has got a dog, a camel and a rhinoceros – she keeps them in the bedroom.

●

When she wants to go to the toilet, she goes outside.

●

She was in a singing group called 'Queen'.

If I were the Queen, I'd sit on my throne all day.
Elizabeth Budd, aged 5, from Hemel Hempstead

The Queen lives in Windsor – in a castle. She has a cooked breakfast every day, is very posh and drinks wine.
Natalie Glew, aged 8, from Lincolnshire

Barrymore: *If you were the Queen, what would you do?*
Lucy: *I would lie in bed all day and eat cherries.*
Lucy Ryan, aged 6, from Jedburgh

Serhad Firat, aged 6

The Queen orders her servants to get her something to eat.
Callum Weston, aged 7, from Yeovil

Luisa Valencio, aged 6

The Queen is important. She wears a crown and a long skirt, sits in a chair and calls for her knights to fight dragons and stuff. For breakfast she has Queen Puffs, milk and a spoon of sugar, and she drinks Sunny Day Orange.
Liam Colmer, aged 6, from Waterlooville

The Queen sends people letters when they get to 100.
Kate Burrows, aged 6, from Havant

The Queen sits around on her throne, ordering people about: 'Get me some grapes.'
Tiffany Whitchurch, aged 7, from north Somerset

The Queen of England lives in a huge palace with fountains, and slides for children. She has bacon, egg, sausages, beans on toast and orange juice for breakfast, and steak, turkey, peas, spaghetti, gravy, pud and cakes.
Jake Thomas, aged 8, from Cardiff

Daniel Ryan Hill, aged 6

And what about Parliament...?

Barrymore: *What does the Prime Minister do?*
Joseph: *Collects money.*
Barrymore: *And what does he do with it?*
Joseph: *He buys houses, and jets and stuff.*
Joseph Anderson, aged 6, from Liverpool

Tony Blair has to make peace with government when they have a big argument.
Callum Weston, aged 7, from Yeovil

Tony Blair is the Governor of Wales and does important things for the Prime Minister and delivers messages.
Jake Thomas, aged 8, from Cardiff

Tony Blair is the Prime Minister – the Boss of England.
Natalie Glew, aged 8, from Lincolnshire

I think the Prime Minister is Mr Lionel Blair.

•

The Prime Minister couldn't live in the Houses of Parliament, 'cos he couldn't pay the rent.

•

I think the Houses of Parliament is where Michael Barrymore lives and Queen Elizabeth works.

•

I watch MPs on television and they're all chatterboxes.

•

The Lords wear wigs on their heads like Lily Savage.

•

America is about ten minutes from London.

•

The President of America lives in a white horse.

When I Grow Up...

Time was when boys wanted to be engine drivers and girls wanted to be nurses. But times have changed...

Shahin, aged 6

I want to be a roadsweeper – it's the greatest thing in the world.
Natasha Greene, aged 5, from Harrow Weald

Barrymore: *What do you want to be?*
Matthew: *I want to be a boy that strips off down the street.*
Barrymore: *You mean, like on* The Full Monty?
Matthew: *I do that sometimes on Saturdays and Sundays.*
Matthew Jackson, aged 6

I want to be a cleaner when I grow up. I want to clean in the studio so I can watch you doing your job. So when you get too old, then you can retire. I can take your place.
Jenny Alexander, aged 7, from Lancashire

Sayeeda, aged 6

roßer

policemen

Anas Abu, aged 6

When I grow up, I want to be a man.
Adam Cobb, aged 5, from Scotland

When I grow up, I want to be a shepherd.
Harry Alexander, aged 4, from Preston

I want to be an adult when I grow up so I can be lazy.
Nicole Goodchild, aged 6, from Cockfosters

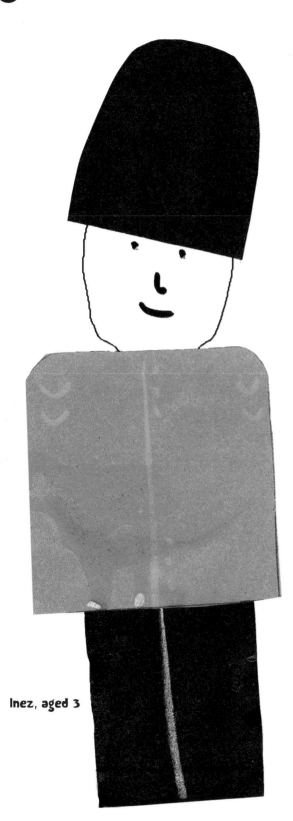

Inez, aged 3

Barrymore: *What do you want to be when you grow up?*
Gareth: *Nothing.*
Gareth Fient, aged 5, from Kent

Jenny has her own money-making idea: *I'm going to steal some from the Queen.*
Jenny Alexander, aged 7, from Lancashire

I want to be a Mummy – not someone wrapped in bandages, but someone with children.
Kate Burrows, aged 6, from Havant

I want to be a nurse so I can make people better and take babies out of people.
Megan Corfield, aged 5, from Swinton

Barrymore: *What do you want to be when you grow up?*
Adam: *A policeman.*
Barrymore: *And have you got any handcuffs at all?*
Adam: *Some toy ones.*
Barrymore: *And has anyone else in the house got any handcuffs?*
Adam: *Me Dad.*
Adam Norton, aged 4

When I'm older I want to be a teacher and boss children around!
Taylor Furneaux, aged 4, from Dagenham

I want to be a policeman so I can arrest people.
Liam Smith, aged 6, from Southampton

I want to be a doctor and a policeman. Policemen put people in handcuffs and then put them in jail, especially people who steal things. Anyone caught stealing should be sent to prison for 15 years.
Samuel Hather, aged 4, from Halifax

Hope Fox, aged 9

I want to be a doctor so I can fix people and open them up and see how they work from the inside. When I am a doctor I am going to open Mum up and check her bones and then stitch her back up again.
Alex Howell, aged 5, from Liverpool

I want to be a police officer so I can arrest people and take them to jail, especially my cousins, who are buggers.
Adam Davies, aged 7, from Liverpool

Halima Miah, aged 6

Michale barymore

Police

police

docter

I'd like a brother when I'm older, called 'Brooklyn Beckham'.
Callum Weston, aged 7, from Yeovil

I want to be Scadger the Badger and fly helicopters and shoot baddies.
Joshua Smeed, aged 5, from Portsmouth

I want to be a woodmaker, so I can make a rowing boat and row to Ireland.
Jake Thomas, aged 8, from Cardiff

I want to be a scarecrow and wear old things because I've never been one ...
Daniel Baines, aged 4, from Ashstead

Shilpy Begum, aged 6

Stars In Their Eyes

How impressed are kids by stars...?

michaelBanymory

Left: Danny Shore,
aged 8

Riyad Hussain, aged 6

Television stars only come out at night.

•

Cilla earns about £5.29 a week.

•

Stars eat champagne and they eat burgers.

•

You can never throw vegetables in stars' faces.

Huw Williams, aged 9

When you're a star, no one can tell you to shut up.

•

Madonna's a star – she lives in a caravan.

•

David Beckham's toilet is made out of gold.

•

Michael Barrymore sleeps in his tidy bed and eats sausages.

I don't like Posh Spice, 'cos you can see her bones when she is dancing. But Britney Spears is a sexy babe.
Tom Bird, aged 6, from Cardiff

Barrymore: *Is there anybody on telly your Dad likes? A favourite actress?*
Sophie: *You.*
Sophie Zumbe, aged 7

Mona, aged 6

Steve

Heaven
And
Earth

**What goes on
in Heaven?
Come on our
guided tour...**

Steve West, aged 6

Barrymore: *What does God look like?*
Jake: *He's got old rags on.*
Jake MacDonald, aged 6, from Salford

Barrymore: *Who lives in
Heaven?*
Tyronne: *God and King James I.
The Studors were before that.*
**Tyronne Alexander-Jarrett,
aged 7, from London**

Mimi, aged 3

*God looks like Jesus and flies
around the world making
things.*
**Samuel Hather, aged 4,
from Halifax**

*God has a beard as big as me
and a loud voice.*
**Natalie Glew, aged 8,
from Lincolnshire**

*God lives in Heaven with
polystyrene on the sides. He's got
a plant with leaves for a hat,
dark brown eyes, nice lips, wears
a white dress and has wings.*
**Jake Thomas, aged 8,
from Cardiff**

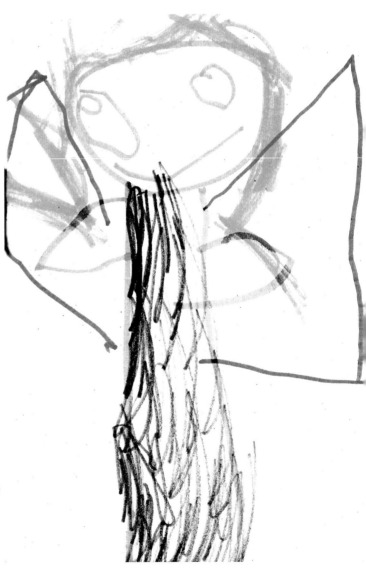

Mounder Sotehi, aged 6

Barrymore: *Do you know who Jesus is?*
Adam: *A man.*
Barrymore: *And what did Jesus do?*
Adam: *Fly.*
Barrymore: *He flies?*
Adam: *He's up in the sky.*
Adam Cobb, aged 5, from Scotland

In olden times they thought Mars was a hot and bothered planet, but it's just like Edinburgh really.
Robert Beaumont, aged 6, from Edinburgh

Preston means if somebody's hair's sticking up then they can come there.
Harry Alexander, aged 4, from Preston

Paege-Ryan Murray, aged 6

Barnaby Platt, aged 9

Right: Kevin Frost, aged 7

Jayne Fredericks, aged 7

Barrymore: *What's the difference between Jamaica and this country?*
Tyronne: *In Jamaica, it's hotter. And if you're white, you could turn black.*
Tyronne Alexander-Jarrett, aged 7, from London

We went to the Wailing Wall in Israel. The men were standing there, praying. My Nan said, 'Isn't it disgusting? It's terrible that!' She thought they were having a wee on the wall ...
Mark Williamson, aged 8, from Cheshire

Sometimes I daydream in class and go to a place where everything is pink.
Natalie Chua, aged 7, from Bletchley

Barrymore: *Where are you from?*
Dominic: *England.*
Barrymore: *And what number England are you from?*
Dominic: *36.*
Dominic Moore, aged 5

Rowena Brown, aged 7

Angel

Trivial Pursuits

There's nothing like an interesting hobby...

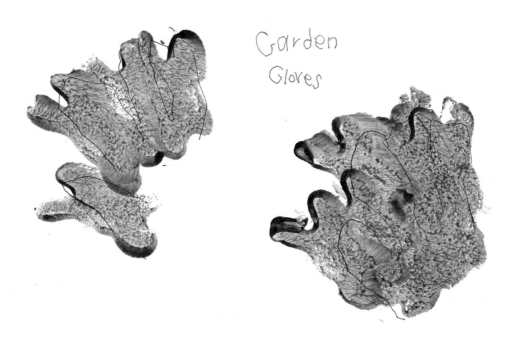

Garden Gloves

Top: Lucy Clayton, aged 5
Bottom: Gus Allen, aged 6

Mimi, aged 3

Barrymore: *What's your favourite football team?*
Adam: *George.*
Adam Cobb, aged 5, from Scotland

Barrymore: *Does your Dad play rugby? He looks like a rugby player.*
Rhys: *He used to, but now he's got a hard ear.*
Rhys Hodnett, aged 7, from Cardiff

Danny Shore, aged 8

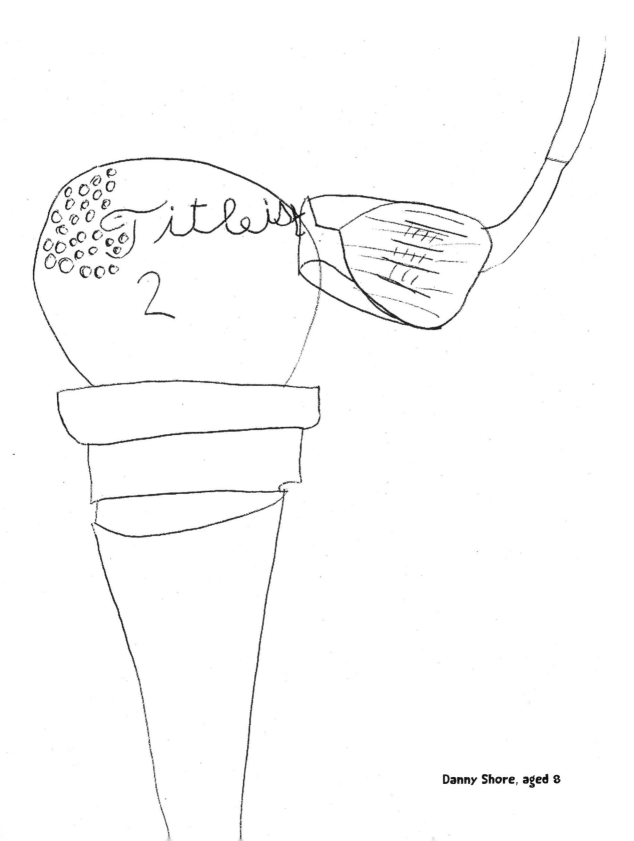

Danny Shore, aged 8

Flora Bourne, aged 6

Mich'el Bamymore

Sonya, aged 6

Roy, **aged 7**

Barrymore: *What do you like watching on TV, Jessica?*
Jessica: Coronation Street.
Barrymore: *And who's your favourite on Coronation Street?*
Jessica: *Vera.*
Barrymore: *And do you like Hayley?*
Jessica: *She's a boy.*
Jessica Martin, aged 7, from Croydon

I would like to have special powers so I can control Mum and Dad, and make them do exactly as I want.
Kate Burrows, aged 6, from Havant

I collect dinosaurs because they eat people.
Vincent Riley, aged 4, from Hove

David, aged 6

Danny Shore, aged 8

HULK HOGAN

Tara Morris, aged 10

Hospitals

Kids give their diagnosis on hospitals...

Dockter

Thamina Yeasmin, aged 6

- *Florence Nightingale was a nurse and started hospitals.*

- *Florence Nightingale was in* **The Magic Roundabout.**

Dad

Michael Barrymore

Neema, aged 6

- *When you break your bones, you mend it with glue.*

- *Doctors don't train – they practise on patients.*

Policeman

Mum

Imran Ahmed Jobber, aged 6

Dad

Doctorr

- *Sometimes Mummy and Daddy play Doctors and Nurses at home.*

- *If you get knocked down by a car, you have to go to the nearest phone box and phone 999.*

Danny Shore, aged 8

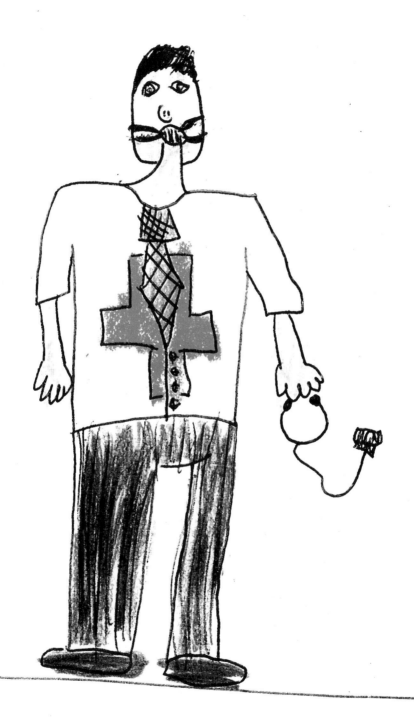

Danny Shore, aged 8

The Clothes Show

**Kids are really
fashion-conscious
these days.**

**It's a pity they can't
say the same
about some of
their families...**

Claire Norman, aged 7

Devante, aged 6

Sara, aged 5

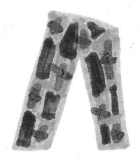

Danny Shore, aged 8

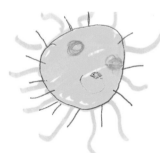

Toby, aged 5

Jayne
Fredericks,
aged 7

Michael Bamymore.

dum

Shat hair

tall

✓ismart

nosty

Michael Bamymore is Funny.
He is dum.
Michael Bamgmore is nasty
He is smart.

Naima Begum, aged 6

Robert: *Nanny's pads make it look like she's got boobs on her shoulders.*
Barrymore: *What are boobs?*
Robert: *Dangly things.*
Robert Betts, aged 7, from Ashford

Kevin Frost, aged 7

Sana Babar, aged 6

James, aged 6

Elvis
Presly

Barrymore: *Does Daddy ever wear a kilt?*
Liam: *Yes.*
Barrymore: *And does he wear anything underneath the kilt?*
Liam: *T-shirt and jumper.*
Liam Wilkinson, aged 4, from Scotland

Mum says that if you go out looking trampy, then everyone will laugh at you.
Aisha Weise-Forbes, aged 7, from Plumstead

Mum had a dream once. Her knickers were too big.
Chantelle Douglas, aged 8, from Bristol

Mum has hairy legs, which she shaves with a machine.
Jake Thomas, aged 8, from Cardiff

I like pretty dresses and it takes 100 hours to do my hair.
Ria St Hilaire, aged 5, from Middlesex

Mum is trying to lose her belly fat so she can pierce her belly button.
Ben Russell, aged 7, from Leeds

Barrymore: *What do you think about body-piercing?*
Christopher: *It's wicked. When I'm older I want two earrings with a chain going up to my nose and then from my nose down to my belly button.*
Christopher Walsh, aged 10, from Mitcham, Surrey

When Mummy puts weave in her hair, she looks like a princess. But when she doesn't, she looks like a real terror.
Charli-Patryce Williamson, aged 6, from London

My little brother Kieran can't fold his jumper properly. Only I can.
Liam Wilkinson, aged 4, from Scotland

My sister leaves all her knickers lying on the floor.
Bobby Burgess, aged 8, from London

Chris Jones, aged 7

Likes
And
Dislikes

Kids have the
funniest likes
and dislikes...

Lucy Clayton, aged 5

Hugo, aged 5

Lucy Clayton, aged 5

Dog

Helena, aged 6

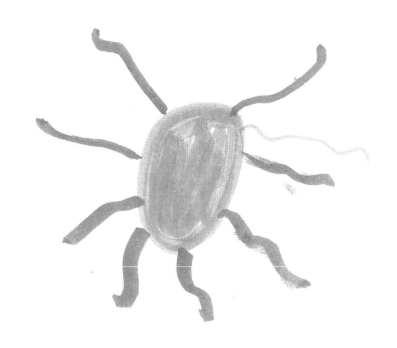

Darren, aged 6

I love the colour black – I like the way it is made.
Kate Burrows, aged 6, from Havant

My best friend is Ben, but sometimes he breaks up with me, 'cos he calls me names like 'Burger Face'.
Liam Colmer, aged 6, from Waterlooville

I like playing on my computer, trains 'cos they are always moving, and when my Mum cuddles me.
Adnam Turner, aged 6, from Luddesdowne

I hate going to the toilet. It is such a nuisance when you're watching a film or a video and you have to miss the middle bits.
Aimee Reynolds, aged 5, from Wakefield

I hate my Dad kissing my Mum before me ...
Whitley-Ruth Chadwick-Heyes, aged 5, from Accrington

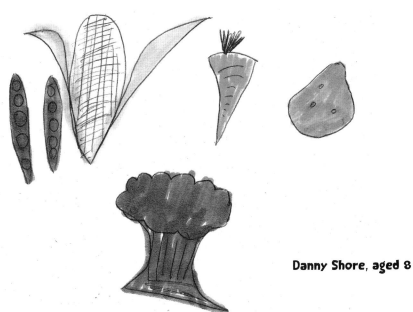

Danny Shore, aged 8

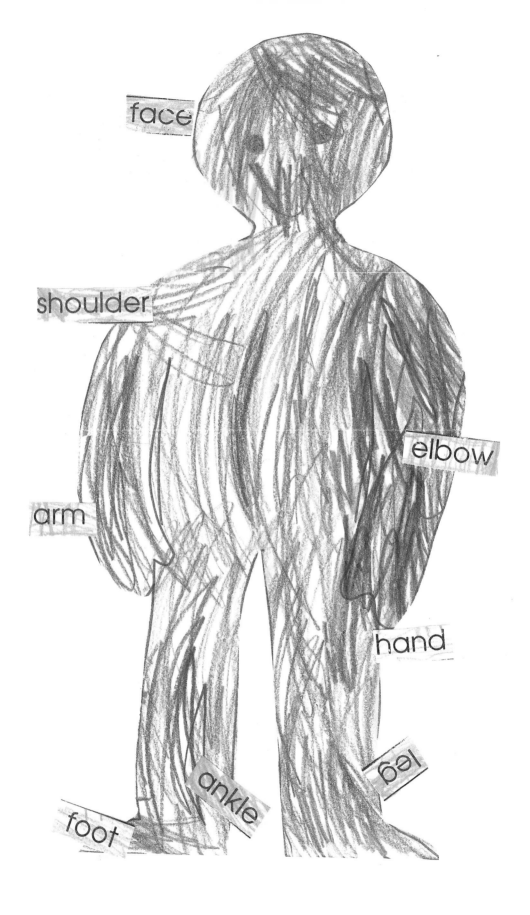

Wise Beyond Their Years

Words of wisdom and philosophy from the under-10s branch of MENSA...

Alison Smith, aged 3

Barrymore: *Where do diamonds come from?*
Mariella: *Treasure Island.*
Mariella Hiscock, aged 5, from Chesterfield

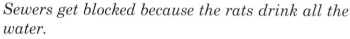

We're all made out of old stars.
Robert Beaumont, aged 6, from Edinburgh

*Your brains are all lines and pink, and they
control your body, they do.*
Peri Ozkeskin, aged 7, from Essex

*Sewers get blocked because the rats drink all the
water.*
Alex Howell, aged 5, from Liverpool

**Hannah Thomas,
aged 14 months**

A judge arrests people and will put them in jail.
Dylan Davis, aged 6, from Sheffield

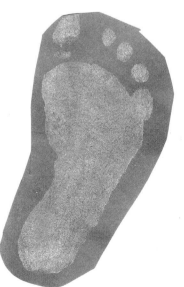

*If you leave things in the freezer for five
years they go rotten.*
Alicia Jauffret, aged 5, from London

Good manners are important, otherwise you would not get any sweets.
Clayton Fernley, aged 6, from Milton Keynes

Barrymore: *Jessica, we've got a bit of a problem here ...*
Jessica: *Just hurry up and spit it out.*
Jessica Martin, aged 7, from Croydon

Barrymore: *What's your favourite food?*
Anthony: *Carrots.*
Barrymore: *Do you like beans?*
Anthony: *No way – they make you fart!*
Anthony Duffy, aged 6, from Liverpool

Barrymore: *What do you think about life?*
Christopher: *There's no point living. You're only going to die.*
Christopher Walsh, aged 10, from Mitcham, Surrey

Barrymore: *What's the worst thing you've ever done?*
Gareth: *The worst thing I've ever done is come on here.*
Gareth Fient, aged 5, from Kent

ACKNOWLEDGEMENTS

The *Kids Say The Funniest Things* team would like to thank very much the following schools for their co-operation and help in making the vox pop items for the programme and for their delightful pictures:

Newington Green Primary School; Vernessa Assanah, Charlotte Mumford, Natasha Brown, Mellanie Morgan, Fahmida Azad, Sibel Hudaverdi, Tien Huy Nguyen, Mandeep Singh, Hassan Khatouli, Ilyas Sevik, Devante Adams, Sibel Hudaverdi, Isobel Lane-Rogans, Daniel Roberts, Keturah Innis, Duygu Sedan Hozman, Azanya Byer-Andrews, Emma Elizee, Mehmet Ganidagli, Yesmin Akdag, Jefferson Tomaya, Stephen Hoang, Callum Isaac, Ryan Finnegan, Nazrui and Rene.

Blue Gate Fields Primary School; Sufian Karino, Monisha Sahni, Farhana Paruin, Sana Babar, Dilwar Hussain, Imran Ahmed Jobber, Mohima Akthar, Thamina Yeasmin, Hafsa Khanom, Nasima Begum, Shanaz Khan, Riyad Hussain, Halima Miah, Mizanur Rahman Masum, Saima Begum, Farhan Islam, Anas Abu, Shilpy Begum, Saqiq Ahmed Kiaz, Nazmin, Marian, Aysha, Aysha J, Juned, Nabilah, Mai, Sayeeda, Neema and Shahin.

Hungerford Primary School; Samuel Adewunmi, Natalia Remolina, Serhad Firat Ginkd, Bao The Khud, Kimberly Wilson, Michelle Elizabeth Hinojosa Bastidas, Jade Lennox, Luisa Valencio, Charlie Watkin, Daniel Ryan Hill, Alan McKenna, Abdi, Rhys English, Anu Olukoga, Paege-Ryan Murray, Billy Allsep, Mounder Sotehi, Jack Atherton, Clyde Hughes, Tianna Nicholls, Morgan Boon, John Jair Escobar, Alice Lillie Batten, Harley Derrick, Maryam Butt, James Russell, Manish Maharjan, Brogan Jones, Hannah Arbon, Mona, Johnn, Jodie and Lucas.

Joseph Lancaster Primary School; Orry Newell-Holman, Curtis Gayle, Blessing Olayiwola, Drewry Reynolds-Tieku, Tanrayo Makinde, Karl Jones, Juan Camilo Lopez Gazzon, Jashun Brown, Fatimah Adegoke, Aboul Hassan, Ajibade Gbemisola, Segum Oyenuga, Jobed Ali, Yewande Salawe, Deborah Abban-Mensah, Ayo Lawal, Rubina Begum, Olaoluwa Ukim, Naima Begum, Julia Barnes, Ibrahim Mohamed, Sonya, Jaswan, Roy and Lee.

St. George's CE Primary School, Clun; Joe Haddigan, Florence Kerry, Samantha Connelly, Polly Williams, Tara Hinton, Elizabeth Weaver, Jessica Haddigan, Gus Allen, Stephanie Thomas, Fiona Johnston, Avanghan Jennifer Watkins, Heidi Luckhurst, Lotte Allen, Hope Fox, Huw Williams, Barnaby Platt, Ned Rawlings, Tara Morris, George Cunning and Caitlin Allen.

We would also like to thank the following children for their lovely pictures: Lucy Clayton from Cirencester, Flora Bourne from Kentish Town, Danny Shore from Walthamstow, Mimi, Helena and Inez Buchanan from Battersea, and thanks also to the children who sent in pictures from the Premier Nursery and Montessori School, Uxbridge.

We would like to thank all those children who came to the many auditions up and down the country but never, on this occasion, made it onto the programme. Special thanks also to all the parents and guardians of the children.

Finally we would like to thank all the children involved in making the programmes, for without their particular views on the world we wouldn't have *Michael Barrymore's Kids Say The Funniest Things*.